# Launching Your Dream: A Beginner's Guide to Starting Your Own Business

Antoinette Kleinhans

# Launching Your Dream: A Beginner's Guide to Starting Your Own Business

## Table Of Contents

| | |
|---|---|
| Chapter 1: Introduction to Entrepreneurship | 2 |
| Chapter 2: Exploring Business Ideas | 4 |
| Chapter 3: Understanding Business Models | 7 |
| Chapter 4: Low-Cost Startup Strategies | 10 |
| Chapter 5: Creating Your Business Plan | 12 |
| Chapter 6: Legal Considerations for Startups | 14 |
| Chapter 7: Setting Up Your Online Presence | 17 |
| Chapter 8: Funding Your Startup | 20 |
| Chapter 9: Launching Your Business | 22 |
| Chapter 10: Measuring Success and Growth | 25 |
| Chapter 11: Overcoming Challenges | 27 |
| Chapter 12: Looking to the Future | 30 |

# Launching Your Dream: A Beginner's Guide to Starting Your Own Business

## Chapter 1: Introduction to Entrepreneurship

### The Entrepreneurial Mindset

The entrepreneurial mindset is the cornerstone of any successful business endeavor. It embodies a unique blend of traits, attitudes, and approaches that empower individuals to identify opportunities, take calculated risks, and navigate the challenges of starting and growing a business. For beginners, cultivating this mindset is essential as it will guide them through the complexities of entrepreneurship. An open and adaptable mindset encourages learning from failures, which can often serve as valuable lessons in the journey of launching a business.

At the heart of the entrepreneurial mindset is a strong sense of curiosity and a passion for problem-solving. Entrepreneurs often see the world through a lens of possibilities, constantly seeking gaps in the market where they can offer innovative solutions. This proactive approach drives them to explore various online business models, whether it's e-commerce, digital services, or affiliate marketing. By embracing a mindset that welcomes experimentation, beginners can discover which model resonates best with their skills and interests, paving the way for a fulfilling business venture.

Resilience is another vital characteristic of the entrepreneurial mindset. The path to starting a business is rarely smooth, and setbacks are inevitable. Beginners must understand that challenges are part of the entrepreneurial journey. Those who possess resilience can bounce back from failures and setbacks, learning and adapting their strategies along the way. Developing this quality allows aspiring entrepreneurs to maintain their focus and motivation, even when faced with obstacles, ultimately leading them closer to their goals.

Moreover, effective goal-setting is a key aspect of the entrepreneurial mindset. Setting clear, achievable goals allows beginners to create a structured path for their business journey. This involves breaking down larger ambitions into smaller, manageable tasks, which can help maintain momentum and track progress. A well-defined business plan serves as a roadmap, enabling entrepreneurs to visualize their objectives and the steps necessary to reach them. This strategic approach not only minimizes overwhelm but also enhances accountability and motivation.

Lastly, networking and collaboration are crucial elements of the entrepreneurial mindset. Building relationships with other entrepreneurs, mentors, and industry experts can provide invaluable insights and support. Beginners should actively seek opportunities to connect with others in their field, whether through online forums, social media, or local business events. These connections can lead to partnerships, collaborations, and new ideas that enrich the entrepreneurial journey. By fostering a mindset that values relationships and community, aspiring business owners can create a robust support system that contributes to their long-term success.

### Identifying Your Passion and Skills

# Launching Your Dream: A Beginner's Guide to Starting Your Own Business

Identifying your passion and skills is a crucial step in the journey of starting your own business. This process not only helps you discover what truly excites you but also aligns your entrepreneurial endeavors with your strengths. Begin by reflecting on activities that energize you, whether they are hobbies, volunteer work, or past job experiences. Consider moments when you felt particularly engaged or fulfilled. Jot down these instances, as they may reveal underlying passions that can fuel your business idea.

Next, assess your skills objectively. Take stock of both hard and soft skills you possess. Hard skills might include technical abilities, such as graphic design or coding, while soft skills encompass communication, leadership, and problem-solving. Create a list of your skills and seek feedback from friends, family, or colleagues who can provide insights into your strengths. This external perspective can illuminate talents you may have overlooked. Understanding your skill set will allow you to leverage these abilities effectively in your business.

After identifying your passions and skills, consider how they intersect. A Venn diagram can be a helpful visual tool for this exercise. In one circle, list your passions; in the other, your skills. The overlapping area will highlight potential business ideas that resonate with both your interests and capabilities. This intersection is where your most authentic business opportunities lie, as it combines what you love with what you excel at. Pursuing a business idea from this vantage point increases the likelihood of long-term satisfaction and success.

Moreover, exploring online resources and communities can further aid in this discovery process. Join forums, attend workshops, or participate in networking events focused on entrepreneurship. Engaging with like-minded individuals can provide inspiration and expose you to different perspectives on how to channel your passions and skills into viable business models. Additionally, online courses can help you hone specific skills or gain new ones that are relevant to your entrepreneurial aspirations.

Finally, remember that identifying your passion and skills is an ongoing journey. As you progress in your business, you may uncover new interests or develop additional skills. Stay open to evolution and be willing to adapt your business model as you grow. Embracing this dynamic process will not only enhance your personal development but also ensure your business remains relevant and fulfilling. By taking the time to identify what you are passionate about and what you do best, you will lay a solid foundation for a successful and sustainable business venture.

## Overcoming Common Fears

Fear is a natural response when embarking on the journey of starting a business. Many beginners grapple with specific anxieties, such as the fear of failure, the fear of financial instability, and the fear of not being taken seriously. Recognizing these fears is the first step toward overcoming them. It is essential to understand that every successful entrepreneur has faced similar challenges. The key is to reframe these fears as opportunities for growth and learning rather than insurmountable obstacles.

# Launching Your Dream: A Beginner's Guide to Starting Your Own Business

One of the most common fears is the fear of failure. This fear can be paralyzing, preventing individuals from taking the necessary steps to launch their business. To combat this, it is beneficial to adopt a mindset that views failures as stepping stones rather than endpoints. Each setback can provide valuable insights and lessons that can be applied to future endeavors. By setting realistic goals and acknowledging that mistakes are a part of the entrepreneurial journey, beginners can build resilience and confidence, making it easier to move forward despite setbacks.

Financial concerns often weigh heavily on aspiring entrepreneurs. The fear of losing money can deter many from pursuing their business ideas. To alleviate this fear, it is crucial to create a clear and detailed business plan. A well-structured plan not only outlines the steps needed to achieve business goals but also includes financial projections, potential costs, and revenue forecasts. By understanding the financial landscape and preparing for various scenarios, beginners can feel more secure in their decisions and less anxious about potential financial pitfalls.

Another prevalent fear is the worry about being taken seriously in a competitive market. Beginners may doubt their expertise and wonder if they can compete with established businesses. To counter this fear, it's important to focus on unique strengths and the value that one can bring to the market. Building a strong personal brand and leveraging social media can enhance visibility and credibility. Networking with other entrepreneurs and seeking mentorship can also provide support and encouragement, reinforcing the belief that everyone has something valuable to contribute, regardless of experience level.

Lastly, fear of the unknown can hinder progress. Many aspiring business owners are uncertain about where to begin or how to navigate the complexities of starting a business. Embracing a learning mindset and seeking knowledge through workshops, online courses, and resources can empower beginners. The more informed individuals are about different business models and strategies, the more equipped they will be to tackle challenges head-on. By taking small, actionable steps and continually educating themselves, entrepreneurs can build confidence and gradually diminish their fears, paving the way for a successful business launch.

# Chapter 2: Exploring Business Ideas

## Brainstorming Business Concepts

Brainstorming business concepts is a vital step in the entrepreneurial journey, allowing aspiring business owners to explore their passions, skills, and market opportunities. This process involves generating a wide array of ideas, which can later be refined into viable business models. To begin, it is essential to create an environment that encourages creativity and open-mindedness. Consider setting aside dedicated time for brainstorming, free from distractions, and gather a diverse group of individuals to contribute different perspectives. Engaging with friends, family, or potential customers can lead to insights that you may not have considered on your own.

# Launching Your Dream: A Beginner's Guide to Starting Your Own Business

One effective technique for generating business ideas is to identify problems or gaps in the market. Think about everyday challenges you or others face and how a product or service could address these issues. This approach not only helps in discovering potential business concepts but also ensures that your idea has a built-in demand. Furthermore, analyzing trends within your areas of interest can reveal emerging opportunities. Look into sectors that are gaining traction, such as sustainability, health and wellness, or remote work solutions, and consider how you can position yourself within these growing industries.

Another method for brainstorming business concepts is to leverage your own skills and experiences. Reflect on your background, whether it's professional expertise, hobbies, or personal interests, and explore how these can translate into a business. For instance, if you have a knack for graphic design, you might consider starting an online service to help small businesses enhance their branding. Alternatively, if you are passionate about cooking, a meal prep service could be a viable option. The intersection of your skills and market needs can often lead to unique and fulfilling business ideas.

As you generate ideas, it is crucial to evaluate their feasibility and alignment with your goals. Not every concept will be suitable for your situation, so take the time to research potential markets, competition, and startup costs. This assessment will help you narrow down your ideas to the most promising ones. Consider creating a simple business model canvas to outline key aspects such as target customers, value propositions, and revenue streams. This will not only clarify your thinking but also provide a framework for developing a more detailed business plan later on.

Lastly, remember that brainstorming is an iterative process. It is perfectly normal for ideas to evolve or even change as you delve deeper into research and planning. Stay open to feedback and be willing to adapt your concepts based on insights from your target audience or industry experts. Networking with other entrepreneurs and attending workshops can further enrich your understanding and inspire new directions. By fostering a mindset of exploration and adaptability, you will be well on your way to developing a solid business concept that resonates with both you and your future customers.

## Researching Market Demand

Researching market demand is a crucial step in the journey of launching your own business. Understanding the needs and preferences of your potential customers can significantly influence the direction and success of your venture. Begin by identifying your target audience. This involves determining who will benefit from your products or services, their demographics, and their specific interests. Conducting surveys, interviews, or focus groups can provide valuable insights into what your audience truly desires and the gaps your business can fill in the market.

Once you have a clear picture of your target audience, utilize online tools and resources to analyze market trends and consumer behavior. Websites like Google Trends can reveal what topics are currently popular and how interest in them fluctuates over time. Additionally, social media platforms serve as a goldmine for understanding consumer sentiment and preferences. By observing discussions and trends within relevant online communities, you can gather qualitative data that complements your quantitative research.

# Launching Your Dream: A Beginner's Guide to Starting Your Own Business

Incorporate competitor analysis into your market research to assess demand for similar products or services. Identify your direct competitors and evaluate their offerings, pricing strategies, and customer feedback. This information will not only help you understand the current market landscape but also highlight areas where you can differentiate your business. By recognizing what competitors do well and where they fall short, you can fine-tune your business model to better meet customer needs.

It is also essential to validate your ideas before fully committing to your business concept. This can be achieved through methods such as creating a minimum viable product (MVP) or conducting a pilot program. These approaches allow you to test your concept in real-world conditions and gather feedback from early adopters. By analyzing this data, you can make informed adjustments to your business strategy, ensuring that it aligns with genuine market demand.

Finally, continuously revisiting and adapting your market research is vital as you progress with your business. Markets are dynamic, and consumer preferences can change rapidly. Establishing a system for ongoing research will help you stay ahead of trends and maintain a competitive edge. Whether through regular customer surveys or keeping an eye on industry reports, being proactive in understanding market demand will help you make strategic decisions that foster growth and sustainability for your business.

## Evaluating Your Ideas

Evaluating your ideas is a critical step in the journey of starting your own business. This process involves assessing the viability and potential of your concepts in a realistic manner. Begin by conducting thorough market research to understand your target audience and the competitive landscape. This research will help you identify gaps in the market that your business could fill, as well as potential challenges you may face. Look for trends in consumer behavior and preferences, as these insights can guide you toward ideas that resonate with your audience.

Next, consider the practicality of your ideas in terms of resources and skills. As a beginner, it's essential to align your business concept with your existing capabilities or be prepared to acquire new skills. Evaluate whether you have the necessary tools, knowledge, and support to bring your idea to fruition. This introspection will help you determine if your idea is not only innovative but also feasible within your current circumstances. Keep in mind that low-cost startup strategies can play a significant role in this evaluation, as they allow you to test your ideas without significant financial risk.

After assessing the market and your resources, it's time to analyze the financial aspects of your ideas. Create a preliminary financial plan that outlines potential costs, pricing strategies, and revenue projections. This financial analysis will help you understand the economic viability of your business concept. It is crucial to be realistic and conservative in your estimates to avoid overextending yourself. Understanding the financial implications will also aid you in determining the best online business model, as different models have varying cost structures and revenue potentials.

# Launching Your Dream: A Beginner's Guide to Starting Your Own Business

Furthermore, seek feedback from trusted peers, mentors, or potential customers. Engaging with others can provide you with diverse perspectives that you may not have considered. This external input can highlight strengths and weaknesses in your ideas, allowing you to refine them further. Constructive criticism can be invaluable, as it can point out potential pitfalls and areas for improvement. Join forums or local business groups where you can share your ideas and gain insights from those who have successfully navigated similar challenges.

Finally, maintain an open mind throughout the evaluation process. Be willing to pivot or adapt your ideas based on the information you gather. Flexibility is key to entrepreneurship, as the business landscape can change rapidly. The goal should be to arrive at a well-rounded, viable business concept that not only excites you but also meets the needs of your target audience. By thoroughly evaluating your ideas, you lay a solid foundation for launching your business and increase your chances of long-term success.

## Chapter 3: Understanding Business Models

### Overview of Online Business Models

In the digital age, online business models have transformed the way entrepreneurs approach their ventures. Understanding these models is crucial for beginners looking to start their own business with minimal investment and maximum impact. Each model offers unique advantages and challenges, making it essential for aspiring business owners to explore their options. From e-commerce to service-based businesses, the possibilities are vast and varied, allowing individuals to align their skills and passions with market demand.

E-commerce is one of the most recognized online business models, characterized by selling products directly to consumers through a digital storefront. This model can take various forms, including dropshipping, where the entrepreneur sells products without holding inventory, or print-on-demand services, which allow for customized items without upfront costs. For beginners, e-commerce presents a low-cost entry point, requiring only a website and a marketing strategy to attract customers. With the right niche and marketing tactics, newcomers can carve out a profitable space in the online marketplace.

Another popular online business model is the subscription service, which provides customers with recurring access to products or services for a fee. This model fosters customer loyalty and ensures a steady stream of income, making it appealing for entrepreneurs. Subscription boxes, online courses, and membership sites are just a few examples of this approach. For beginners, developing a subscription service can often leverage existing content or resources, thus minimizing the need for significant startup capital. It also encourages ongoing engagement with the audience, which can lead to valuable insights and opportunities for growth.

# Launching Your Dream: A Beginner's Guide to Starting Your Own Business

Service-based businesses have also found a strong foothold online. Freelancing, consulting, and coaching are models where individuals offer their expertise directly to clients. This type of business often requires minimal upfront investment, as the primary cost may involve setting up a professional website and marketing services. For beginners, this model allows for flexibility and scalability, enabling them to start small and gradually expand their offerings based on client demand and feedback. Moreover, the growth of remote work has opened doors for service providers to reach a global audience, significantly increasing their potential customer base.

Lastly, affiliate marketing presents an attractive model for beginners who wish to enter the online business world without creating their own products. In this model, entrepreneurs promote other companies' products or services and earn a commission for each sale made through their referral links. This approach requires a strong online presence, often cultivated through content creation, social media, or email marketing. Affiliate marketing can be started with minimal investment, making it ideal for those looking to test the waters of online business. By strategically selecting profitable niches and building an engaged audience, beginners can establish a sustainable income stream while minimizing financial risk.

## E-commerce vs. Service-Based Models

E-commerce and service-based models represent two distinct paths for aspiring entrepreneurs, each offering unique advantages and challenges. E-commerce, characterized by the sale of physical or digital products via an online platform, provides a scalable and often low-cost avenue for beginners. Entrepreneurs can set up an online store with relative ease, utilizing platforms like Shopify, WooCommerce, or Amazon. This model allows for the potential of passive income, as products can be sold around the clock without the need for direct interaction with customers. Additionally, e-commerce businesses can tap into global markets, significantly expanding their customer base.

In contrast, service-based models focus on delivering intangible offerings such as consulting, coaching, or freelance work. These businesses often require lower initial investments compared to e-commerce, as they may not need extensive inventory or a physical storefront. For beginners, starting a service-based business can be as simple as leveraging existing skills or expertise to attract clients. This model allows for flexibility in terms of work hours and can often lead to a more personal relationship with clients, fostering loyalty and repeat business. However, it typically requires a more hands-on approach and can limit scalability unless the entrepreneur develops systems or hires additional help.

When considering which model to pursue, it is essential to evaluate personal strengths, skills, and interests. E-commerce may suit those who enjoy product development, marketing, and logistics, while service-based models might appeal to individuals who excel in interpersonal communication and problem-solving. Additionally, market research is crucial; understanding consumer demand in your chosen niche can inform whether an e-commerce or service-based approach is more viable. Beginners should also consider their financial situation, as e-commerce often involves upfront costs for inventory and website development, whereas service-based businesses might allow for a more gradual investment in tools and marketing.

# Launching Your Dream: A Beginner's Guide to Starting Your Own Business

Marketing strategies will also differ significantly between these models. E-commerce businesses often rely on digital marketing techniques such as search engine optimization (SEO), pay-per-click advertising, and social media campaigns to drive traffic to their online stores. In contrast, service-based businesses may benefit from networking, referrals, and building a personal brand to attract clients. Social proof, such as testimonials and case studies, becomes vital in the service sector, whereas product reviews and ratings play a more prominent role in e-commerce. Understanding these distinctions can help beginners tailor their marketing efforts effectively.

Ultimately, the choice between e-commerce and service-based models should align with the entrepreneur's vision and lifestyle. Both paths offer opportunities for growth and success, but the decision should reflect an understanding of one's capabilities and market needs. Beginners are encouraged to create a detailed business plan that outlines their goals, target audience, and operational strategies, regardless of the chosen model. This foundational step will not only clarify the business vision but also serve as a roadmap for navigating the complexities of launching and scaling their venture.

## Subscription and Membership Models

Subscription and membership models have gained significant traction in recent years, offering businesses a steady stream of revenue while providing customers with ongoing value. These models can be particularly appealing for beginners looking to start their own business, as they often require lower initial investments and can be adapted to various niches. Whether you're considering a digital service, a subscription box, or a membership community, understanding the fundamentals of these models is essential for laying a solid foundation for your business.

At the core of subscription and membership models is the concept of recurring revenue. This stability can ease financial strain, allowing new entrepreneurs to focus on growth rather than constant customer acquisition. By offering products or services on a subscription basis, businesses can cultivate a loyal customer base. This loyalty not only helps in reducing churn rates but also fosters customer engagement, which can lead to upselling or cross-selling opportunities. As a beginner, you can start small, testing your offerings with a limited audience before scaling up based on their feedback and needs.

When developing your subscription or membership model, it's crucial to identify what unique value your offering brings to potential customers. This could mean curating exclusive content, providing specialized services, or delivering unique products that are not readily available elsewhere. By clearly defining your value proposition, you can create compelling marketing strategies that resonate with your target audience. Consider conducting surveys or focus groups to gather insights into what your potential customers are seeking, which can help refine your offerings and enhance customer satisfaction.

Pricing strategies play a vital role in the success of subscription and membership models. As a beginner, it's important to strike a balance between affordability and sustainability. Research your competitors to understand market rates, and consider implementing tiered pricing options to cater to a broader audience. Offering a free trial or a low-cost introductory period can also attract initial customers and encourage them to experience the value of your service before committing long-term. This strategy can help build trust and demonstrate the benefits of your offering.

# Launching Your Dream: A Beginner's Guide to Starting Your Own Business

Finally, maintaining customer relationships is key to the longevity of subscription and membership businesses. Regular communication, personalized experiences, and continuous value delivery will keep your subscribers engaged and reduce the likelihood of cancellations. Utilize feedback loops to understand customer satisfaction and adapt your offerings accordingly. By fostering a community around your brand, whether through forums, social media groups, or exclusive events, you can enhance customer loyalty and create a vibrant ecosystem that supports your business growth.

## Chapter 4: Low-Cost Startup Strategies

### Bootstrapping Your Business

Bootstrapping your business is a powerful approach for aspiring entrepreneurs who want to launch their ventures without relying on external funding. This method emphasizes utilizing personal savings, reinvesting profits, and being resourceful to grow your business from the ground up. For beginners, this can be an empowering way to maintain control over your venture while minimizing financial risks. By fostering a mindset of creativity and frugality, you can develop a sustainable business model that supports your long-term goals.

Starting with a clear business plan is essential for bootstrapping success. A well-structured plan outlines your vision, target audience, and revenue streams, providing a roadmap for your journey. As you create your plan, focus on defining your unique value proposition and how you intend to reach potential customers. This clarity will guide your decision-making process, helping you allocate resources effectively and prioritize tasks that drive growth. Remember, a business plan is not a static document; it should evolve as your business progresses and market conditions change.

Low-cost startup strategies are at the heart of bootstrapping. Identify areas where you can minimize expenses without compromising quality. For example, consider leveraging free or low-cost online tools for marketing, customer relationship management, and project management. Social media platforms offer a cost-effective way to build brand awareness and engage with your audience. Additionally, networking with other entrepreneurs can provide valuable insights and collaborative opportunities, allowing you to tap into shared resources and knowledge without significant financial investment.

Reinvesting profits is a crucial aspect of bootstrapping that can accelerate your business growth. As your venture starts generating revenue, prioritize reinvestment over personal gains. This could mean upgrading your tools, enhancing your marketing efforts, or expanding your product offerings. By channeling profits back into the business, you create a cycle of growth that can lead to increased sales and market presence. This approach not only strengthens your business but also builds a solid foundation for future success.

# Launching Your Dream: A Beginner's Guide to Starting Your Own Business

Finally, bootstrapping fosters resilience and adaptability, which are essential traits for any entrepreneur. As you navigate the challenges of starting a business, you will learn to think critically and make decisions that align with your goals. Embrace the obstacles as learning opportunities and remain open to adjusting your strategies when necessary. With determination and a clear vision, you can successfully bootstrap your business, transforming your dreams into reality while cultivating valuable skills and experiences along the way.

## Leveraging Free Tools and Resources

Leveraging free tools and resources is a crucial strategy for beginners embarking on their entrepreneurial journey. With the digital landscape continually evolving, a wealth of free resources is available to assist aspiring business owners. These tools can help streamline operations, enhance marketing efforts, and manage finances without incurring significant costs. By tapping into these resources, beginners can allocate their limited budgets more effectively while still laying a strong foundation for their business.

One of the first areas to consider is website development. Numerous platforms offer free website builders that enable users to create professional-looking sites without any coding knowledge. Tools like WordPress, Wix, and Weebly provide user-friendly interfaces and customizable templates, allowing you to establish an online presence quickly. A strong website is essential for any online business model, as it serves as your digital storefront where potential customers can learn about your products or services. By utilizing these free tools, you can focus on crafting compelling content and building your brand identity.

In addition to website creation, marketing your business can be a daunting task, especially for those just starting. Fortunately, free social media platforms such as Facebook, Instagram, and Twitter provide an excellent way to connect with your target audience. By creating engaging content and utilizing these platforms' various features, you can build a community around your brand. Additionally, free graphic design tools like Canva allow you to create eye-catching visuals for your marketing campaigns, helping to attract and retain customers without breaking the bank.

Managing finances is another critical aspect of running a business, and there are many free tools available to assist beginners in this area. Software like Wave and ZipBooks offer free accounting solutions that can help you track income and expenses, manage invoices, and generate financial reports. By utilizing these resources, you can gain valuable insights into your business's financial health, allowing you to make informed decisions and plan for growth. A solid understanding of your finances is essential for any startup, and leveraging these free tools can significantly reduce the stress associated with financial management.

Finally, when it comes to creating a business plan from scratch, there are numerous free templates and resources available online. Websites like SCORE and the Small Business Administration provide valuable guides and examples that can help you outline your vision, define your target market, and develop a strategic plan for growth. By utilizing these resources, you not only save time but also ensure that you are following best practices in your business planning process. Leveraging free tools and resources empowers aspiring entrepreneurs to take their ideas from concept to reality with confidence and clarity, setting the stage for long-term success.

# Launching Your Dream: A Beginner's Guide to Starting Your Own Business

## Creative Marketing on a Budget

Creative marketing on a budget is an essential skill for any entrepreneur starting out, especially when resources are limited. Many successful businesses have emerged from innovative marketing strategies that prioritize creativity over financial expenditure. By leveraging available tools and platforms, you can effectively promote your business without breaking the bank. Understanding your target audience and utilizing free or low-cost marketing channels can lead to significant growth while keeping expenses manageable.

One of the most effective ways to engage potential customers is through social media. Platforms like Instagram, Facebook, and Twitter offer free access to millions of users. By creating engaging content that resonates with your audience, you can build brand awareness and foster a loyal community. Focus on storytelling and share behind-the-scenes glimpses of your business journey. User-generated content can also enhance your visibility; encourage satisfied customers to share their experiences and tag your brand to attract new followers.

Networking plays a crucial role in budget-friendly marketing. Attend local events, workshops, and online webinars to connect with other entrepreneurs and potential customers. Building relationships with fellow business owners can lead to valuable collaborations, cross-promotions, and referrals. Utilize platforms like LinkedIn to expand your professional network and share insights about your business. Engaging with your community and industry peers can create word-of-mouth marketing opportunities that are both organic and cost-effective.

Content marketing is another powerful strategy that requires minimal investment. By creating informative blog posts, videos, or podcasts, you can share your expertise and position yourself as a thought leader in your niche. Quality content not only helps educate your audience but also improves your website's search engine optimization (SEO), making it easier for potential customers to find you online. Sharing valuable information fosters trust and credibility, encouraging visitors to choose your business when they are ready to make a purchase.

Finally, consider leveraging email marketing to maintain a connection with your customers. Building an email list allows you to communicate directly with interested prospects and loyal clients. Use newsletters to share updates, promotions, and valuable content that keeps your audience engaged. Many email marketing platforms offer free tiers for beginners, making it an affordable option. By nurturing these relationships, you can turn one-time customers into repeat buyers, ultimately driving sales without significant investment. By implementing these creative strategies, you can effectively market your business while staying within budget.

# Chapter 5: Creating Your Business Plan

## Importance of a Business Plan

# Launching Your Dream: A Beginner's Guide to Starting Your Own Business

A business plan serves as a foundational blueprint for any aspiring entrepreneur. It outlines the vision, objectives, and strategies that will guide a business from inception to growth. For beginners, having a well-structured business plan is essential as it provides clarity on the direction of the business, helping to articulate the goals and the means to achieve them. It acts as a roadmap, allowing entrepreneurs to visualize their journey while identifying potential challenges and opportunities along the way.

Moreover, a business plan is a critical tool for securing funding and attracting investors. Investors and lenders typically require a comprehensive plan that details how their investment will be utilized and the expected return on investment. By presenting a solid business plan, entrepreneurs can demonstrate their commitment, foresight, and understanding of the market, which in turn builds trust and increases the likelihood of obtaining financial support. This is especially pertinent for online business models where clear projections and market analysis can significantly impact funding decisions.

In addition to attracting investments, a business plan aids in establishing a marketing and operational strategy. It compels entrepreneurs to conduct thorough market research, which helps identify target audiences, competitors, and potential challenges. This research not only informs marketing strategies but also influences decisions regarding pricing, product offerings, and distribution channels. For those pursuing low-cost startup strategies, a business plan can pinpoint cost-effective methods for reaching customers and generating revenue, making it a valuable resource for maximizing limited resources.

Furthermore, a business plan encourages accountability and measurement of progress. By setting specific milestones and performance metrics, entrepreneurs can evaluate their progress against their goals. This ongoing assessment allows for adjustments to be made when necessary, ensuring that the business remains agile in a dynamic market environment. Regularly reviewing the business plan helps maintain focus on long-term objectives while adapting to short-term changes, an important aspect for anyone launching a business from scratch.

Finally, the process of creating a business plan itself is beneficial for personal development. It forces aspiring entrepreneurs to think critically about their business concept, challenge their assumptions, and refine their ideas. This reflective practice fosters a deeper understanding of the business landscape and equips entrepreneurs with the knowledge and skills necessary to navigate their path successfully. In essence, a business plan is not just a document; it is a vital tool that empowers beginners to launch their dreams with confidence and strategic insight.

## Key Components of a Business Plan

A well-structured business plan is crucial for any entrepreneur looking to launch a successful venture. The key components of a business plan not only provide a roadmap for the business but also help communicate the vision and strategy to potential investors and stakeholders. Understanding these components will empower you to create a comprehensive plan that addresses all critical aspects of your business.

# Launching Your Dream: A Beginner's Guide to Starting Your Own Business

The executive summary is the first section of the business plan and serves as an overview of your entire document. It should succinctly summarize your business concept, mission statement, target market, and financial projections. This is often the first section that investors will read, so it needs to be compelling and clear. Focus on highlighting what makes your business unique and the potential it has for growth. A strong executive summary sets the tone for the rest of the plan and piques the interest of the reader.

Next, the market analysis provides insight into the industry landscape and your target market. This section should include details about market size, trends, and customer demographics. Analyzing your competitors is also essential here; understand their strengths and weaknesses to identify opportunities for your own business. This information not only informs your marketing strategy but also demonstrates to potential investors that you have a deep understanding of the environment in which your business will operate.

The marketing and sales strategy outlines how you plan to attract and retain customers. This section should describe your branding, pricing strategies, distribution channels, and promotional tactics. For online businesses, detailing your digital marketing approach, such as social media engagement and search engine optimization, is critical. A well-defined marketing strategy can significantly enhance your chances of success by ensuring that you reach your target audience effectively.

Lastly, the financial projections section is where you present your revenue model, funding requirements, and expected financial outcomes. Include detailed forecasts for income, expenses, and cash flow, covering at least three to five years. This information should be grounded in realistic assumptions based on your market analysis. Investors will look closely at this section to assess the viability of your business, so presenting clear and credible financial data is vital. By combining all these components, you will create a robust business plan that serves as a solid foundation for your entrepreneurial journey.

## Writing Your Executive Summary

An executive summary serves as a crucial component of your business plan, acting as a concise overview that captures the essence of your venture. When writing your executive summary, aim to provide a snapshot of your business concept, highlighting your mission, vision, and goals. This section should encapsulate what your business does, the market it serves, and the unique value it brings to potential customers. Keep in mind that this summary is often the first impression investors or stakeholders will have of your business, so clarity and impact are paramount.

Begin by outlining your business idea in a straightforward manner. Describe the product or service you intend to offer, ensuring that you communicate its relevance to your target audience. If you're focusing on an online business model, for instance, detail how your digital offerings will fulfill a specific need or solve a problem for your customers. This clarity will help potential investors understand the core of your business and its potential for success in a competitive marketplace.

# Launching Your Dream: A Beginner's Guide to Starting Your Own Business

Next, emphasize your market analysis. Identify your target market, including key demographics, purchasing behaviors, and any trends that support the viability of your business. Discuss the competitive landscape, highlighting your unique selling proposition and how you differentiate yourself from others in the field. This information will not only reinforce your business concept but also demonstrate that you've done your homework and are prepared to navigate the challenges of starting a new venture.

Financial projections are another essential element of your executive summary. Provide a brief overview of your expected revenue streams, startup costs, and profitability timeline. For low-cost startup strategies, showcase how you plan to manage expenses while maximizing returns. This financial snapshot can reassure potential investors that you have a realistic understanding of your business's financial landscape and are prepared to make informed decisions.

Finally, conclude your executive summary with a call to action. Encourage readers to engage with your business plan further, whether it's to seek investment, partnership, or simply to learn more about your journey. This invitation creates an opening for dialogue and demonstrates your enthusiasm for your business. A well-crafted executive summary not only outlines your business vision but also serves as a powerful tool for generating interest and support, paving the way for your entrepreneurial aspirations.

## Chapter 6: Legal Considerations for Startups

### Choosing the Right Business Structure

Choosing the right business structure is a crucial decision that can significantly impact your startup's success. As a beginner, understanding the various types of business structures available to you is essential. The primary options include sole proprietorships, partnerships, limited liability companies (LLCs), and corporations. Each structure comes with its own set of benefits and drawbacks, which can influence everything from your personal liability to tax obligations. Taking the time to research and evaluate these options will help you make an informed decision that aligns with your business goals and values.

A sole proprietorship is the simplest and most straightforward business structure, often favored by individual entrepreneurs due to its ease of setup and minimal regulatory requirements. As a sole proprietor, you have complete control over your business and keep all profits. However, it's important to note that this structure does not provide personal liability protection, meaning your personal assets could be at risk if your business incurs debt or faces legal issues. This structure is ideal for low-cost startups and online businesses where the owner can operate independently and manage risks effectively.

# Launching Your Dream: A Beginner's Guide to Starting Your Own Business

If you plan to start your business with one or more partners, a partnership may be the right choice. This structure allows you to share responsibilities, resources, and profits with your partners. Partnerships can be general or limited, with varying degrees of liability for each partner. While this structure fosters collaboration and shared expertise, it also requires clear agreements and communication to ensure all partners are on the same page. For beginners, understanding the dynamics of working with partners and establishing a solid partnership agreement is vital to avoid conflicts down the line.

Limited liability companies (LLCs) combine the benefits of both sole proprietorships and corporations. An LLC provides personal liability protection for its owners while allowing for flexible management structures and tax advantages. This option is particularly attractive for beginners looking to establish a low-cost startup with a degree of protection against personal financial risk. Additionally, the LLC structure can accommodate various business models, making it a versatile choice for those exploring online business opportunities or different revenue streams.

Lastly, corporations offer the most protection from personal liability but come with greater complexity and regulatory requirements. For beginners, incorporating might seem daunting due to the costs and paperwork involved. However, if you plan to grow your business significantly, attract investors, or go public, a corporation could be the best long-term choice. Understanding the implications of this structure will help you determine whether the benefits outweigh the challenges for your particular business model. In conclusion, carefully evaluating your goals, resources, and risk tolerance will guide you in selecting the right business structure, setting a solid foundation for your entrepreneurial journey.

## Registering Your Business

Registering your business is a critical step in transforming your entrepreneurial vision into reality. This process not only legitimizes your enterprise but also lays the groundwork for future success. As a beginner, it can seem daunting, but understanding the requirements and steps involved can simplify the process significantly. Each jurisdiction has its own rules, so it is essential to familiarize yourself with local laws and regulations that pertain to business registration.

The first step in registering your business typically involves choosing a suitable business structure. Whether you opt for a sole proprietorship, partnership, limited liability company (LLC), or corporation, each structure has distinct implications for taxes, liability, and operations. For new entrepreneurs, an LLC is often recommended due to its flexibility and protection of personal assets. However, understanding the nuances of each structure will allow you to select the best option for your specific situation and long-term goals.

Once you have decided on a business structure, the next step is to choose a unique business name that resonates with your target audience and aligns with your brand. A memorable name not only helps in marketing but also plays a crucial role in the registration process. After selecting the name, you will need to check its availability through your local business registry. This ensures that your chosen name is not already in use and prevents potential legal issues in the future.

# Launching Your Dream: A Beginner's Guide to Starting Your Own Business

After securing your business name, the actual registration process begins. This usually involves filling out the required forms, paying a registration fee, and submitting your application to the appropriate government agency. Depending on your location, this may be a state, provincial, or local office. It's often advisable to consult with a legal professional or a business advisor during this phase to ensure that all documents are completed accurately and to avoid costly mistakes.

Finally, after registering your business, you will need to obtain any necessary permits or licenses required for your specific industry. This step is crucial as it ensures compliance with local regulations and can affect your ability to operate legally. Additionally, consider setting up a business bank account to separate your personal and business finances. This not only simplifies accounting but also enhances your professional image. With your business registered, you are now equipped to move forward with your entrepreneurial journey, focusing on growth and success in your chosen niche.

## Understanding Licenses and Permits

Understanding the landscape of licenses and permits is crucial for any entrepreneur embarking on the journey of starting a business. These legal requirements vary significantly based on industry, location, and business structure. At the outset, it is essential to comprehend that licenses and permits serve as a means of compliance with local, state, and federal regulations. They not only protect consumers but also ensure that businesses operate within the legal framework of their respective sectors. Ignoring these requirements can lead to penalties or, in severe cases, the closure of your business.

To begin, aspiring business owners should identify the specific licenses and permits relevant to their industry. For example, if you are planning to open a food service establishment, you will likely need health permits and food safety certifications. On the other hand, an online business might require fewer permits, but it could still necessitate a sales tax permit or a business license. Conducting thorough research is key; resources such as the Small Business Administration (SBA) and local chambers of commerce can provide invaluable guidance regarding the necessary documentation for your business.

Once you have identified the required licenses and permits, the next step is to navigate the application process. This can often be a daunting task for beginners, as it may involve filling out a variety of forms, paying fees, and sometimes undergoing inspections. It is advisable to create a checklist that outlines each requirement, deadlines, and associated costs. Staying organized will alleviate some of the stress and ensure that you do not overlook any critical steps. Additionally, consider seeking advice from seasoned entrepreneurs or legal professionals who can offer insights into the process.

The timeline for obtaining licenses and permits can vary widely. Some permits may be granted quickly, while others can take several weeks or even months. This is particularly important to keep in mind when developing your business plan and setting timelines for your launch. Incorporating these timelines into your planning will prevent delays and help maintain your momentum as you prepare to enter the market. It is often beneficial to start this process early, allowing you to address any unforeseen issues that may arise.

# Launching Your Dream: A Beginner's Guide to Starting Your Own Business

In conclusion, understanding licenses and permits is a foundational aspect of launching your business. By dedicating time to research, organizing your application process, and being aware of the timelines involved, you will lay a solid groundwork for your entrepreneurial venture. Embracing these legal requirements not only enhances your credibility but also positions your business for long-term success in a competitive environment. As you navigate this process, remember that diligence and preparation are key to turning your dream into a reality.

## Chapter 7: Setting Up Your Online Presence

### Building a Website on a Budget

Building a website on a budget is an essential step for any aspiring entrepreneur looking to establish an online presence without breaking the bank. With the myriad of tools and resources available today, you can create a professional-looking website that effectively represents your brand and engages potential customers. Understanding what you need and where to allocate your resources can help you launch your business without incurring overwhelming costs.

First, consider the purpose of your website. Are you using it as a portfolio to showcase your work, or do you intend to sell products directly? Clearly defining your website's goals will help you choose the right platform and tools to facilitate those objectives. For instance, if you're looking to create a simple blog or informational site, platforms like WordPress or Wix offer free and low-cost options that are user-friendly. If e-commerce is your focus, consider platforms like Shopify or Squarespace, which provide tailored solutions for online selling, often with low monthly fees.

Next, choose a domain name wisely. A memorable and relevant domain name is crucial for branding and search engine visibility. Many hosting providers offer affordable domain registration services, sometimes even bundled with their hosting packages. Take time to shop around and compare prices, as some providers frequently offer promotional rates for the first year. Additionally, consider using a free email service linked to your domain for professional communication, which can enhance your brand image without added expenses.

Designing your website need not be an expensive endeavor. Many budget-friendly website builders come equipped with templates and drag-and-drop features, allowing you to customize your site without needing advanced technical skills. Utilize free stock images and graphics from websites like Unsplash or Canva to enhance your visual appeal without incurring high costs. If your business requires specific functionalities, explore plugins and add-ons that can be integrated at minimal or no cost, ensuring your site remains functional and attractive.

# Launching Your Dream: A Beginner's Guide to Starting Your Own Business

Finally, once your website is up and running, focus on cost-effective marketing strategies. Leverage social media platforms to drive traffic to your site, engage with your audience, and share valuable content related to your business. Building an email list can also be a low-cost way to communicate directly with your customers and keep them informed about new products or updates. Investing time in search engine optimization (SEO) can further enhance your website's visibility, drawing more visitors without the need for costly advertising campaigns. By implementing these strategies, you can successfully build a website on a budget while laying a solid foundation for your business's growth.

## Utilizing Social Media for Growth

Social media has transformed the way businesses connect with their audience, making it an indispensable tool for growth, especially for beginners. With platforms like Facebook, Instagram, Twitter, and LinkedIn, entrepreneurs can reach potential customers at a fraction of the cost of traditional marketing methods. Understanding how to effectively utilize these channels can significantly enhance your brand visibility, drive traffic to your website, and foster customer relationships. As you embark on your entrepreneurial journey, consider how social media can be integrated into your overall business strategy.

To begin leveraging social media, identify the platforms that align best with your target audience and business goals. Each platform has its unique characteristics and user demographics. For instance, Instagram is ideal for visually-driven brands, while LinkedIn is more suited for B2B interactions. Conduct research to determine where your potential customers spend their time online, and focus your efforts on those platforms. Creating tailored content that resonates with your audience will not only engage them but also establish your brand as a trusted resource in your niche.

Content creation is at the heart of any successful social media strategy. As a beginner, you should aim to produce high-quality, relevant content that showcases your expertise and builds credibility. This can include blog posts, infographics, videos, and live streams. Consistency is key; a regular posting schedule helps keep your audience engaged and informed. Additionally, utilizing storytelling techniques can draw in your audience, making your brand more relatable and memorable. Engaging with your audience through comments and direct messages can also convey that you value their input and are attentive to their needs.

Another effective strategy for growth through social media is collaboration. Partnering with influencers, other businesses, or even fellow entrepreneurs can expand your reach and introduce your brand to new audiences. Consider hosting joint events, giveaways, or co-created content to maximize exposure. These collaborations can be particularly beneficial for low-cost startups, as they can harness the established followings of others to gain traction without significant financial investment. Networking within your niche can open doors to opportunities that might otherwise remain inaccessible.

# Launching Your Dream: A Beginner's Guide to Starting Your Own Business

Finally, track and analyze your social media performance to refine your strategies continually. Utilize analytics tools provided by social media platforms to measure engagement, reach, and conversion rates. Understanding what content performs best will help you make informed decisions and adapt your approach to better serve your audience. By remaining agile and responsive to feedback, you can cultivate a loyal following that supports your business growth. Embracing social media not only aids in building your brand but also fosters a community around your business, paving the way for sustainable success in your entrepreneurial journey.

## Email Marketing Essentials

Email marketing is a powerful tool for entrepreneurs looking to launch their own business. It offers a direct line of communication with potential customers, allowing you to promote your products or services effectively. One of the essentials of email marketing is building a quality email list. This can be achieved by offering valuable content in exchange for email addresses, such as eBooks, newsletters, or exclusive discounts. By focusing on growing a targeted list of subscribers who are genuinely interested in your offerings, you create a foundation for successful email campaigns.

Once you have established an email list, it's crucial to understand the importance of segmentation and personalization. Segmenting your audience based on demographics, purchase history, or engagement level allows you to tailor your messages to different groups. Personalized emails that address the specific needs and interests of your subscribers can significantly increase open and click-through rates. By crafting messages that resonate with your audience, you enhance the likelihood of converting leads into loyal customers.

Crafting compelling content is another essential aspect of email marketing. Your emails should not only inform but also engage and inspire action. Use attention-grabbing subject lines to entice recipients to open your emails, and ensure that your content is concise, valuable, and aligned with your brand's voice. Including clear calls to action guides your readers on what to do next, whether it's making a purchase, signing up for an event, or sharing your content with others. Consistency in your messaging and branding reinforces your identity and builds trust with your audience.

Analyzing and optimizing your email campaigns is vital for continuous improvement. Utilize analytics tools to track key metrics such as open rates, click-through rates, and conversion rates. This data provides insights into what resonates with your audience and what may need adjustment. A/B testing different elements of your emails, such as subject lines, images, or calls to action, can help you determine the most effective strategies. By regularly reviewing and refining your approach based on data, you can enhance the effectiveness of your email marketing efforts.

Finally, compliance with regulations is an essential consideration in email marketing. Familiarize yourself with laws such as the CAN-SPAM Act and GDPR, which govern how businesses can collect and use email addresses. Obtaining explicit consent from your subscribers and providing easy options to unsubscribe are not just best practices; they are legal requirements designed to protect consumer privacy. By adhering to these regulations, you not only avoid potential penalties but also build trust with your audience, fostering long-term relationships that can lead to sustained business growth.

# Launching Your Dream: A Beginner's Guide to Starting Your Own Business

## Chapter 8: Funding Your Startup

### Exploring Funding Options

When embarking on the journey of starting your own business, understanding the various funding options available is crucial. Each funding avenue comes with its own set of advantages and challenges, making it essential for beginners to explore and identify the best fit for their unique business model. Whether you aim to launch an online business or pursue a low-cost startup strategy, knowing where to seek financial support can greatly influence your venture's success.

One of the most common sources of funding is personal savings. This approach allows you to maintain full control over your business without incurring debt or giving up equity. However, it also entails a significant risk, as you are investing your hard-earned money. It is important to assess your financial situation and determine how much you can afford to invest without jeopardizing your personal finances. By starting small and reinvesting profits back into the business, you can gradually grow your venture while minimizing financial strain.

Another viable option for funding is seeking assistance from family and friends. This route can provide the initial capital needed to launch your business while often coming with more flexible repayment terms compared to traditional lenders. However, it is imperative to approach this option with caution. Clear communication about your business plan, potential risks, and repayment expectations is vital to maintaining healthy relationships. Consider drafting a simple agreement outlining the terms of the investment to prevent misunderstandings down the line.

For those looking for more structured funding, small business loans can be a practical choice. Many financial institutions offer loans designed specifically for startups, which can provide the necessary capital for purchasing inventory, equipment, or marketing efforts. Before applying, it is essential to develop a solid business plan that outlines your goals, target market, and financial projections. This plan will not only help you secure funding but also serve as a roadmap for your business's growth.

Lastly, consider exploring crowdfunding as an innovative funding solution. Platforms like Kickstarter and Indiegogo allow entrepreneurs to present their ideas to the public and receive financial support from interested backers. This method not only provides funding but also serves as a way to validate your business concept and build a community of early supporters. Crafting a compelling pitch and offering attractive rewards in exchange for contributions can significantly enhance your chances of success. By diversifying your funding sources, you can create a more resilient financial foundation for your business.

### Crowdfunding Basics

# Launching Your Dream: A Beginner's Guide to Starting Your Own Business

Crowdfunding has emerged as a revolutionary way for entrepreneurs to raise funds for their business ventures. At its core, crowdfunding involves gathering small amounts of money from a large number of people, typically via online platforms. This method not only helps in collecting the necessary capital but also serves as a valuable marketing tool. For beginners, understanding the fundamentals of crowdfunding is crucial, as it can significantly impact the early stages of their business development.

There are different types of crowdfunding, each serving unique purposes and audiences. Donation-based crowdfunding allows individuals to contribute to a cause without expecting anything in return, making it ideal for charities or community projects. Reward-based crowdfunding, on the other hand, offers backers a tangible reward or product in exchange for their financial support. Equity crowdfunding enables investors to acquire a stake in the business, which can be attractive for startups looking for substantial investments. Understanding these models will help you choose the right approach based on your business goals and the level of commitment you can offer to your backers.

When planning a crowdfunding campaign, a well-crafted business plan is essential. Your plan should clearly outline your business idea, target market, funding goals, and how you intend to use the raised funds. Transparency is key; potential backers want to know exactly how their contributions will help your business grow. Additionally, incorporating a detailed marketing strategy into your business plan is vital. This could include social media promotion, email marketing, and reaching out to relevant communities to generate interest and support for your campaign.

Creating an engaging campaign page is another important aspect of crowdfunding. Your page should tell a compelling story that resonates with potential backers. High-quality visuals, such as images and videos, can significantly enhance your presentation and convey your vision more effectively. Clearly outlining the benefits of your product or service and providing attractive rewards will also motivate people to contribute. Remember, successful crowdfunding is not just about asking for money; it's about building a community around your idea and fostering a sense of involvement among your supporters.

Finally, once your crowdfunding campaign is live, active engagement with your backers is crucial. Regular updates about the progress of your project, milestones achieved, and future plans will keep your supporters invested in your journey. Communication fosters trust and encourages further sharing of your campaign within their networks. Whether your campaign meets its funding goal or not, the relationships built during this process can provide invaluable support as you move forward with launching your business. Embracing the crowdfunding process can be a rewarding experience that not only secures funding but also lays the groundwork for a loyal customer base.

## Managing Your Finances

# Launching Your Dream: A Beginner's Guide to Starting Your Own Business

Managing your finances is a critical aspect of launching your own business, especially for beginners. A solid financial foundation can mean the difference between success and failure. Start by creating a comprehensive budget that outlines your expected income and expenses. This will serve as your roadmap as you navigate the early stages of your business. Consider all potential costs, including materials, marketing, and operational expenses. By having a clear picture of your financial landscape, you can make informed decisions and identify areas where you can save or invest wisely.

Establishing a separate business bank account is essential for maintaining financial clarity. This separation helps you track your business expenses more accurately and makes it easier to manage cash flow. Additionally, it simplifies tax preparation, as you will have all your business transactions in one place. Choose a bank that offers low fees and services tailored to small businesses, ensuring that your banking relationship supports your financial goals rather than hinders them.

When it comes to funding your startup, explore low-cost startup strategies that minimize your initial investment. Consider using personal savings, crowdfunding, or seeking small business grants. Each option has its advantages and drawbacks, so weigh them carefully based on your business model and financial needs. If you're planning to operate an online business, leverage digital tools and platforms that can help you launch without significant overhead costs. Utilizing free or low-cost marketing channels, such as social media, can also help you build your brand while keeping expenses in check.

Creating a solid business plan is another crucial step in managing your finances effectively. This plan should include detailed financial projections, such as revenue forecasts and break-even analysis. Not only does this provide you with a clear financial target, but it also helps attract potential investors or lenders who want to see a well-thought-out strategy for profitability. Revisit and revise your business plan regularly, as your financial situation and market conditions will likely evolve over time.

Lastly, keep a close eye on your financial health by monitoring key performance indicators (KPIs). Track metrics such as cash flow, profit margins, and customer acquisition costs to assess the viability of your business. Regularly reviewing these figures will allow you to identify trends and make necessary adjustments to your strategy. By staying proactive in managing your finances, you can ensure that your business remains on a path toward sustainability and growth, setting yourself up for long-term success.

## Chapter 9: Launching Your Business

### Creating a Launch Plan

# Launching Your Dream: A Beginner's Guide to Starting Your Own Business

Creating a launch plan is a critical step in transforming your business idea into a reality. A well-structured launch plan serves as a roadmap, guiding you through the essential stages of starting your business and ensuring that you have considered every crucial element before going live. Begin by defining your objectives clearly. What do you want to achieve with your launch? Whether it's generating a specific amount of revenue, acquiring a set number of customers, or establishing your brand presence, having clear goals will help you measure your success and adjust your strategies as needed.

Next, identify your target audience. Understanding who your potential customers are will allow you to tailor your marketing strategies effectively. Conduct market research to gather insights into their preferences, behaviors, and pain points. This information will not only help you craft a compelling value proposition but also guide your messaging and promotional tactics. By knowing your audience intimately, you can create a launch that resonates with them and encourages engagement from the outset.

Budgeting is another crucial component of your launch plan. As a beginner, it's essential to be mindful of your expenses and identify low-cost startup strategies that maximize your resources. Create a detailed budget that outlines all anticipated costs, including marketing, website development, and operational expenses. Consider leveraging free or low-cost tools and platforms to minimize expenses. By keeping a close eye on your budget, you can ensure that your launch is financially sustainable and set the stage for future growth.

Your marketing strategy will be the backbone of your launch plan. Determine the channels that will be most effective for reaching your target audience, such as social media, email marketing, or content marketing. Develop a timeline for your marketing activities, ensuring a consistent presence leading up to the launch date. Create engaging content that highlights your unique selling proposition and builds anticipation. A well-executed marketing strategy will help draw attention to your business and drive initial sales or sign-ups.

Finally, establish a feedback loop for post-launch evaluation. After your launch, it's vital to assess what worked and what didn't. Collect feedback from customers and analyze your sales data to identify trends and areas for improvement. This evaluation will provide valuable insights that can inform future marketing strategies and product offerings. By continuously refining your approach based on real-world feedback, you can enhance your business's performance and adapt to changing market conditions, ensuring long-term success.

## Building Buzz Before Launch

Building anticipation for your business launch is crucial to ensure a successful debut. A well-thought-out buzz-building strategy can create excitement and drive early interest in your product or service. Start by identifying your target audience and understanding their needs and preferences. This foundational knowledge will help you tailor your messaging and outreach efforts, ensuring that your promotional activities resonate with potential customers. Focus on creating a compelling value proposition that clearly communicates what makes your business unique and how it can address your audience's pain points.

# Launching Your Dream: A Beginner's Guide to Starting Your Own Business

Social media platforms are invaluable tools for generating buzz before launching your business. They allow you to engage directly with your audience, share your vision, and create a community around your brand. Start by selecting the platforms that best align with your target demographic. Regularly post content that highlights your journey, shares behind-the-scenes glimpses of your product development, and sparks conversations. Consider using polls, contests, or giveaways to encourage interaction and build excitement. The more your audience feels involved in your journey, the more likely they are to support your launch.

Email marketing can also be a powerful asset in your pre-launch strategy. Building an email list before your official launch gives you a direct line to interested customers. Offer incentives, such as exclusive content or early access to your product, to encourage sign-ups. Craft engaging newsletters that provide updates on your progress, share valuable insights related to your niche, and reinforce your brand's mission. This consistent communication not only keeps your audience informed but also fosters a sense of connection and loyalty, making them more likely to convert when your business officially opens.

Collaborating with influencers or bloggers in your industry can amplify your reach and credibility. Identify individuals whose audiences align with your target market and propose mutually beneficial partnerships. This could include guest blog posts, social media takeovers, or joint giveaways. By leveraging their established platforms, you can introduce your brand to new potential customers who may not have discovered you otherwise. Authentic endorsements from trusted voices can significantly enhance your brand's visibility and attractiveness.

Finally, consider hosting a pre-launch event, either virtually or in-person, to create excitement and generate buzz. This could be a live Q&A session, a sneak peek of your product, or even a workshop related to your business's mission. Such events allow for direct interaction with potential customers, giving them a taste of what to expect and why they should be invested in your launch. Encourage attendees to share their experiences on social media, further extending your reach. By effectively building buzz before your launch, you set a solid foundation for your business's success.

## Post-Launch Strategies

Post-launch strategies are essential for ensuring that your newly established business not only survives but thrives in the competitive landscape. After the excitement of launching, it can be easy to fall into a routine and neglect the next steps. To build momentum, focus on refining your value proposition and continuously engaging with your target audience. Regularly revisit what makes your offering unique and how it addresses the needs of your customers. This ongoing evaluation will help you stay relevant and responsive to market changes, setting a solid foundation for growth.

Another critical element in your post-launch strategy is customer feedback. Actively seeking opinions from your initial customers can provide invaluable insights into your product or service. Create avenues for feedback, such as surveys, social media polls, or direct conversations. Use this information not only to improve your offerings but also to foster a sense of community around your brand. When customers see that their input leads to tangible changes, they are more likely to become loyal advocates for your business, spreading the word and helping you attract new clients.

# Launching Your Dream: A Beginner's Guide to Starting Your Own Business

Marketing efforts should also evolve after your launch. Analyze the effectiveness of your initial marketing strategies and be prepared to pivot or adapt based on performance metrics. Utilize digital marketing tools to track user engagement and conversion rates, allowing you to refine your approach. Consider employing low-cost marketing techniques, such as content marketing, social media engagement, and email newsletters, to maintain visibility without straining your budget. By consistently promoting your business and showcasing your expertise, you can build credibility and attract a wider audience over time.

Networking should remain a priority in your post-launch phase. Building relationships with other entrepreneurs, industry professionals, and potential collaborators can open doors to new opportunities. Attend industry events, join online forums, and engage with others in your niche. These connections can lead to partnerships that enhance your offerings, provide mentorship, or even generate referrals. By nurturing these relationships, you not only grow your professional network but also create a support system that can help navigate the challenges of running a business.

Lastly, focus on setting long-term goals to guide your business's growth trajectory. Establish measurable objectives, both financial and operational, that align with your vision. Regularly review these goals to track progress and make adjustments as needed. Implementing a strategic plan will keep you on course and help you prioritize efforts that drive growth. By remaining adaptable and responsive to both successes and setbacks, you can position your business for continued success in the ever-evolving marketplace.

## Chapter 10: Measuring Success and Growth

### Setting Key Performance Indicators

Setting Key Performance Indicators (KPIs) is a crucial step in launching your business, as they provide a measurable way to track progress and success. KPIs serve as the benchmarks against which you gauge your performance, allowing you to assess whether your business strategies are effective. For beginners, understanding how to set relevant KPIs can be the difference between achieving your goals and falling short. It is essential to start with clear, specific objectives that align with your overall business vision.

When establishing KPIs, begin by identifying your primary business goals. These goals could range from increasing revenue and expanding your customer base to improving customer satisfaction or enhancing product quality. Each goal should be SMART—Specific, Measurable, Achievable, Relevant, and Time-bound. For example, instead of a vague objective like "increase sales," a more effective KPI would be "increase online sales by 20% in the next quarter." This clarity will help you stay focused and motivated.

# Launching Your Dream: A Beginner's Guide to Starting Your Own Business

Next, determine which metrics will best measure your progress toward these goals. Depending on your business model, these metrics may include sales figures, website traffic, conversion rates, or customer retention rates. For an online business, you might track metrics like bounce rate and average session duration on your website. Low-cost startups might focus on metrics that assess cost efficiency, such as customer acquisition cost or return on investment for marketing campaigns. Choosing the right metrics is essential; they should provide insight into your business performance without overwhelming you with data.

Regularly reviewing your KPIs is vital to ensure they remain relevant and aligned with your business strategy. As your business evolves, your goals and the market landscape may change, necessitating adjustments to your KPIs. Set a routine, such as monthly or quarterly reviews, to analyze these indicators. This practice not only helps you stay on track but also allows you to celebrate milestones and identify areas where you may need to pivot or refine your approach.

Finally, share your KPIs with your team or stakeholders if applicable. Transparency fosters a sense of accountability and encourages everyone involved to work toward common objectives. When team members understand the metrics that define success, they are more likely to contribute positively to the business's growth. By establishing clear KPIs and fostering a culture of performance evaluation, you lay a solid foundation for your business's success, ensuring that you are not only launching your dream but also steering it toward sustained achievement.

## Analyzing Customer Feedback

Analyzing customer feedback is an essential process for any entrepreneur looking to refine their business model and enhance their offerings. It serves as a direct line of communication between you and your customers, providing valuable insights into their experiences, preferences, and pain points. By systematically collecting and analyzing this feedback, you can identify trends, gauge customer satisfaction, and make informed decisions that align with market demands. This practice not only fosters customer loyalty but also positions your business for sustainable growth in a competitive landscape.

To effectively analyze customer feedback, it's important to establish clear goals for what you hope to learn. Start by determining the specific areas of your business you want to evaluate, whether it's product features, customer service quality, or overall user experience. Utilize multiple channels to gather feedback, including surveys, social media interactions, and online reviews. This diverse approach ensures a comprehensive understanding of customer sentiment and helps you capture a wide array of opinions. By prioritizing the most relevant feedback, you can focus your efforts on the areas that will yield the greatest improvement.

Once you have collected customer feedback, the next step is to categorize and analyze the data. Use qualitative and quantitative methods to identify recurring themes and patterns. For instance, you might discover that many customers appreciate a particular feature of your product while expressing frustration over a different aspect. Tools like spreadsheets or specialized software can assist in organizing this data, allowing you to visualize trends and draw actionable conclusions. This analysis should inform your strategic decisions, guiding you in making adjustments that enhance customer satisfaction and drive business success.

# Launching Your Dream: A Beginner's Guide to Starting Your Own Business

In addition to identifying areas for improvement, analyzing customer feedback also provides an opportunity to celebrate your successes. Positive feedback can highlight the strengths of your business model and reinforce what you are doing well. This recognition not only boosts your confidence but can also serve as a marketing tool. Sharing testimonials and success stories can help build your brand's credibility and attract new customers. By balancing the analysis of both positive and negative feedback, you create a comprehensive view of your business's performance.

Finally, make it a regular practice to revisit and reassess customer feedback. The market is dynamic, and customer preferences can shift over time. Establishing a routine for collecting and analyzing feedback ensures that you remain responsive to your customers' evolving needs. Incorporating this practice into your business operations fosters a culture of continuous improvement, helping you adapt and thrive in an ever-changing marketplace. By valuing customer input and using it to inform your decisions, you not only enhance your offerings but also build a loyal customer base that will support your business for years to come.

## Adjusting Your Business Strategy

Adjusting your business strategy is a crucial step in ensuring the longevity and success of your venture. As a beginner, it's important to remain flexible and responsive to the ever-evolving market conditions. This adaptability can mean the difference between thriving and merely surviving in the competitive landscape. By regularly evaluating your business plan and the outcomes of your strategies, you can identify areas for improvement and growth, allowing your business to pivot effectively when necessary.

When assessing your business strategy, start by gathering data on your performance metrics. This includes understanding your sales figures, customer feedback, and market trends. Utilizing tools such as surveys and analytics can provide valuable insights into how your business is perceived and where it may be falling short. By analyzing this information, you can pinpoint strengths to build upon and weaknesses that require adjustment. This data-driven approach ensures that your decisions are grounded in reality rather than assumptions, thereby increasing your chances of success.

In addition to internal assessments, keep an eye on external factors that may necessitate a shift in strategy. Changes in consumer behavior, technological advancements, and economic fluctuations can all impact your business. For instance, if you notice a growing demand for online services in your niche, it may be time to enhance your online presence or explore digital marketing strategies. Staying informed about industry trends and competitor actions can help you anticipate changes and react proactively, ensuring that your business remains relevant and competitive.

Moreover, consider the importance of feedback from your customers and team members. Engaging with your audience can provide insights that data alone may not reveal. Encourage open communication through forums, social media, or direct interactions to understand their needs and preferences better. Similarly, tapping into the insights of your team can lead to innovative ideas for improvement. Collaboration can foster a culture of continuous improvement, where every member feels valued and empowered to contribute to the success of the business.

# Launching Your Dream: A Beginner's Guide to Starting Your Own Business

Finally, remember that adjusting your business strategy is not a one-time event, but an ongoing process. As your business grows and the market evolves, regularly revisiting your strategy will help you stay aligned with your goals and responsive to changes. Establish a routine for reviewing your business plan and performance, and be willing to adapt as necessary. Embracing this mindset will not only enhance your business's resilience but also position you for sustainable growth in the long run.

## Chapter 11: Overcoming Challenges

### Common Startup Challenges

Starting a business can be an exhilarating journey, but it is often fraught with challenges that can test the resolve of even the most passionate entrepreneurs. One of the most common hurdles faced by new business owners is the lack of a clear and actionable business plan. Many beginners underestimate the importance of this foundational document, which serves as a roadmap for their business. A well-crafted business plan outlines goals, identifies target markets, and lays out strategies for achieving success. Without it, entrepreneurs may find themselves navigating blindly, making costly mistakes that could have been avoided with proper planning.

Another significant challenge is securing adequate funding. New entrepreneurs frequently struggle to find the necessary capital to launch and sustain their businesses. This is especially true for those pursuing low-cost startup strategies, where limited funds require creative solutions. It is crucial for beginners to explore various funding options, including personal savings, loans, grants, and crowdfunding. By diversifying their funding sources and understanding the financial landscape, aspiring business owners can alleviate some of the pressure associated with financial constraints.

Marketing is another area where many new business owners face difficulties. Establishing a brand presence in a crowded marketplace can be daunting for beginners who lack marketing experience. Developing a clear value proposition and identifying the right channels to reach potential customers are essential steps in creating effective marketing strategies. Online business models offer numerous opportunities for reaching audiences at a lower cost, such as social media marketing and content creation. By leveraging these tools, new entrepreneurs can build their brand and engage with customers more effectively.

Time management presents yet another challenge for startups. Entrepreneurs often find themselves wearing multiple hats, juggling various responsibilities that can become overwhelming. The ability to prioritize tasks and delegate when necessary is vital for maintaining productivity and focus. Utilizing tools and software for project management can streamline operations and help new business owners allocate their time more efficiently. By developing strong organizational habits, entrepreneurs can navigate the demands of their startup while ensuring they remain aligned with their long-term goals.

# Launching Your Dream: A Beginner's Guide to Starting Your Own Business

Finally, adapting to change and embracing resilience is crucial for overcoming common startup challenges. The business landscape is dynamic, and unforeseen obstacles will inevitably arise. Beginners must be prepared to pivot their strategies, respond to market shifts, and learn from setbacks. Cultivating a mindset that views challenges as opportunities for growth can empower entrepreneurs to thrive in the face of adversity. By staying adaptable and maintaining a positive outlook, new business owners can build a strong foundation for their ventures and ultimately achieve their dreams.

## Developing Resilience

Developing resilience is an essential skill for anyone embarking on the journey of starting a business. The path to entrepreneurship is often fraught with challenges, from financial uncertainties to market fluctuations and unexpected setbacks. Embracing resilience allows you to navigate these obstacles with a positive mindset, turning potential failures into opportunities for growth. It is not just about bouncing back from difficulties but also about learning from experiences and becoming stronger in the face of adversity.

To cultivate resilience, it is crucial to adopt a proactive mindset. This begins with setting realistic expectations for your business journey. Understand that failures and challenges are not signs of inadequacy but rather integral parts of the learning process. By anticipating potential hurdles, you can prepare yourself mentally and strategically to tackle them head-on. This preparation fosters a sense of control and confidence, enabling you to approach obstacles with a solution-oriented attitude rather than one of defeat.

Another vital aspect of developing resilience is building a robust support network. Surrounding yourself with mentors, peers, and other entrepreneurs can provide invaluable guidance and encouragement. Sharing experiences with others who understand the entrepreneurial landscape can help you gain new perspectives and insights. Engaging with a community, whether online or locally, can serve as a reminder that you are not alone in your struggles and that others have successfully navigated similar challenges.

In addition to external support, nurturing your internal resources is equally important. This involves taking care of your physical and mental well-being through practices such as regular exercise, mindfulness, and stress management techniques. A healthy body and mind contribute to greater resilience by enhancing your ability to cope with stress and make sound decisions. Incorporating self-care routines into your daily life can recharge your energy and clarity, making it easier to face the demands of entrepreneurship.

Lastly, resilience is strengthened through a commitment to continuous learning. Embrace a mindset of curiosity and openness to new ideas, strategies, and feedback. Analyzing what works and what doesn't in your business allows you to adapt and evolve. By viewing challenges as learning opportunities and remaining flexible in your approach, you position yourself to innovate and grow. This adaptability not only enhances your resilience but also increases your chances of long-term success in your entrepreneurial endeavors.

## Seeking Support and Mentorship

# Launching Your Dream: A Beginner's Guide to Starting Your Own Business

Seeking support and mentorship is a pivotal step for any budding entrepreneur. As you embark on your journey to launch a business, the guidance and encouragement of experienced individuals can make a significant difference. Mentorship provides not only knowledge but also valuable insights into the nuances of running a business. Engaging with mentors allows you to tap into their experiences, learn from their successes and failures, and avoid common pitfalls that new entrepreneurs often face. This support can be instrumental in building your confidence and refining your business ideas.

One effective way to seek mentorship is by leveraging local business networks and online platforms. Many organizations, such as SCORE, offer free mentorship programs where experienced business professionals volunteer their time to help new entrepreneurs. Additionally, social media platforms like LinkedIn can be powerful tools for connecting with industry leaders and potential mentors. When reaching out, be clear about your goals and what you hope to achieve from the relationship. A well-articulated request can open doors and invite valuable conversations.

Joining entrepreneurial groups or communities can also provide a wealth of support. These networks often host workshops, seminars, and networking events, enabling you to meet like-minded individuals who share your passion and drive. Engaging with peers offers not only camaraderie but also opportunities for collaborative learning. In these spaces, you can exchange ideas, share resources, and find accountability partners who can help keep you on track as you work towards your business goals.

Additionally, consider seeking out formal mentorship programs offered by local universities or business incubators. Many institutions have initiatives designed to support startups and entrepreneurs, providing access to seasoned professionals who can offer guidance tailored to your specific needs. These programs often include structured curricula that cover essential topics such as business planning, financing, and marketing strategies, ensuring that you receive well-rounded advice as you navigate the complexities of starting a business.

Lastly, don't underestimate the power of informal mentorship. Sometimes, the best advice comes from unexpected sources. Friends, family, or colleagues who have experience in business can serve as valuable sounding boards. Engage them in conversations about your ideas and plans. Their diverse perspectives can illuminate aspects of your business that you may not have considered. By cultivating a support system that encompasses both formal and informal relationships, you can create a robust network that empowers you on your entrepreneurial journey.

## Chapter 12: Looking to the Future

### Planning for Long-Term Success

Planning for long-term success is a crucial aspect of launching any business. As a beginner, it may be tempting to focus solely on immediate gains and quick wins. However, a sustainable business requires a vision that extends beyond the initial stages. This involves setting clear, achievable goals that align with your long-term aspirations. By envisioning where you want your business to be in five or ten years, you can create a roadmap that guides your daily decisions and strategies.

# Launching Your Dream: A Beginner's Guide to Starting Your Own Business

One of the first steps in planning for long-term success is developing a comprehensive business plan. This document not only outlines your business model and market analysis but also includes strategies for growth and sustainability. As you create your plan, be sure to consider your target audience, potential challenges, and competitive landscape. A solid business plan serves as a foundational tool that helps you stay focused and organized as you navigate the complexities of entrepreneurship.

Incorporating flexibility into your long-term strategy is essential. The business landscape is constantly evolving, and being adaptable allows you to respond to changes and new opportunities effectively. Establish regular intervals to review and adjust your business strategies based on market trends and customer feedback. This proactive approach ensures that you remain relevant and competitive, which is vital for sustaining growth over time.

Building a strong network is another key element of planning for long-term success. Surround yourself with mentors, fellow entrepreneurs, and industry professionals who can provide valuable insights and support. Networking not only opens doors to new opportunities but also fosters collaboration and innovation. Engaging with others in your field can help you stay informed about best practices and emerging trends, allowing you to make informed decisions that benefit your business.

Finally, prioritize financial planning as part of your long-term strategy. Establishing a budget, tracking expenses, and forecasting revenue are essential practices that will help ensure your business remains financially healthy. Consider setting aside funds for reinvestment and growth, as well as for unexpected challenges. By maintaining a strong financial foundation and planning for future expenses, you will position your business for sustained success and longevity in the marketplace.

## Scaling Your Business

Scaling your business is a critical step that can elevate your startup from a small operation to a thriving entity. The process typically begins with a solid foundation, which includes a well-defined business plan that outlines your vision, goals, and the strategies you intend to use. For beginners, this means not just having a plan that details your initial offerings but also one that anticipates future growth. Consider what resources you will need, how you will manage increased customer demand, and the potential challenges that may arise as you scale. A comprehensive business plan will serve as your roadmap and help you evaluate your progress along the way.

Once you have established a strong business plan, focus on leveraging technology to streamline operations. Many online business models allow for automation, which can significantly reduce labor costs and improve efficiency. For instance, using e-commerce platforms can help automate inventory management and customer service processes, allowing you to focus on strategic growth activities. Additionally, utilizing digital marketing tools can enhance your outreach and customer engagement, making it easier to attract and retain clients. Adopting these technologies not only saves time and money but also positions your business for scalability.

# Launching Your Dream: A Beginner's Guide to Starting Your Own Business

Building a strong brand presence is another essential aspect of scaling your business. As you grow, it's important to maintain consistency in your branding and messaging across all platforms. This helps in establishing trust and recognition among your target audience. You can achieve this by crafting a unique value proposition that clearly communicates what sets your business apart. Engage with your customers through social media and gather feedback to refine your offerings. A loyal customer base will not only support your initial growth but also advocate for your brand, making it easier to reach new audiences.

Financial management plays a crucial role in scaling your business effectively. Beginners often underestimate the importance of cash flow management. As your business grows, your expenses may increase, and without careful planning, you could find yourself in a tight spot. Create a financial model that projects future revenues and expenses. Explore low-cost startup strategies, such as utilizing freelancers or virtual assistants, to keep overheads low while you scale. It's advisable to keep your personal and business finances separate and consider seeking advice from a financial professional to ensure you are making informed decisions.

Finally, don't hesitate to seek mentorship or join entrepreneurial communities. Surrounding yourself with experienced business owners can provide invaluable insights and support as you navigate the complexities of scaling your venture. Networking can open doors to partnerships, funding opportunities, and valuable advice that can help you avoid common pitfalls. Remember, scaling your business is not just about increasing profits; it's about creating a sustainable operation that can adapt to changes in the market and continue to thrive in the long term.

## Continuing Your Education as an Entrepreneur

Continuing your education as an entrepreneur is essential for staying relevant and competitive in today's fast-paced business environment. As you embark on your entrepreneurial journey, it is crucial to recognize that learning does not stop once your business is launched. In fact, ongoing education can significantly enhance your skills, broaden your knowledge, and introduce you to new ideas that can help you adapt to changing market conditions. Embracing a mindset of lifelong learning not only empowers you but also positions your business for long-term success.

One effective way to continue your education is through online courses and webinars tailored specifically for entrepreneurs. Platforms like Coursera, Udemy, and LinkedIn Learning offer a vast array of courses covering various aspects of business, from marketing strategies to financial management. By investing time in these resources, you can acquire new skills and insights that directly apply to your business model. This approach is particularly advantageous for online business models, where trends and technologies evolve rapidly, requiring entrepreneurs to remain agile and informed.

Networking with other entrepreneurs and industry professionals is another valuable educational opportunity. Joining local business groups, attending workshops, or participating in online communities can provide you with a wealth of knowledge and experience. Engaging with peers allows you to share challenges and solutions, gain different perspectives, and learn from the successes and failures of others. These connections can also lead to mentorship opportunities, where seasoned entrepreneurs can offer guidance and advice tailored to your specific business needs.

# Launching Your Dream: A Beginner's Guide to Starting Your Own Business

Reading books, articles, and case studies related to entrepreneurship and your specific niche is a simple yet effective way to enhance your knowledge base. By immersing yourself in the experiences of others, you can gain insights into best practices and innovative strategies. Make it a habit to set aside time each week to read about industry trends, successful startups, and the latest research in entrepreneurship. This ongoing education not only informs your business decisions but also inspires creativity and innovation in your own ventures.

Finally, consider seeking formal education through business courses or degree programs. Many universities offer part-time or online options that allow you to balance your studies with your entrepreneurial pursuits. A structured educational environment can provide a solid foundation in essential business principles, while also encouraging critical thinking and problem-solving skills. Regardless of the path you choose, prioritizing your education as an entrepreneur will ultimately empower you to build a resilient and thriving business that can weather the challenges of the ever-evolving marketplace.

www.ingramcontent.com/pod-product-compliance
Lightning Source LLC
Chambersburg PA
CBHW041944240526
45473CB00033B/515